Camping Cookbook

Cast-Iron Skillet Recipes

Louise Davidson

ISBN 9798537197386

Printed in the United States

CONTENTS

COOKING WITH CAST-IRON SKILLETS

Are you looking for exciting camp cooking? If yes, then you are in the right place. The culture of camp cooking started in America, but now it is very popular in all western countries.

We all know that as soon as the winter starts, the first thought that comes to mind is to explore the outdoors to the fullest by doing camping trips with our family. This camping cookbook would make a great gift to give an outdoor adventurer. We all find camp cooking very exciting just because of the outdoor environment. It's a great way to enjoy your favorite dishes with food, fire, and fun outside your home.

You will find camp cooking very easy because all you need is some small equipment and some ready-to-use food items. You can make mouthwatering dishes and create great food memories with your family and friends.

We have included 75 easy-to-follow recipes with step-by-step instructions and mouthwatering photos. This cookbook presents categories of recipes from classic breakfasts to party dinner hits and snacks, desserts, and side dishes that require only basic tools and accessible ingredients.

They have all been tried and tested outdoors, and they are all easy to make without compromising on your taste and sophistication. You can make them in a cast-iron skillet which is easy to clean. With this single iron skillet, your camping kitchen setup is almost done—isn't that exciting?

Cooking with a cast-iron skillet can be as simple as you want it to be, and the best part is you can make all these dishes with a maximum of five to six ingredients only.

The cast-iron skillet is one of the sturdiest cooking skillets you'll ever come across. It has been with us for a long time. It can withstand and evenly distribute very high heat. This results in a stronger flavor – the flavor you can't get from cooking in a non-stick skillet – and a shorter cooking time.

Unlike modern skillets which are made non-stick by synthetic linings, cast-iron skillets or skillets can be treated or "seasoned" to become non-stick naturally. The cast-iron skillet adsorbs flavors every time it's used, giving dishes a richer, more complex flavor. This skillet can last a lifetime – as long as it's treated right. It's something that you can pass down to your children and grandchildren.

A Bit of History

Anything made by pouring molten iron into a mold is called cast-iron. Cast-iron was first used way back around 513 BC. The technology originated in China, where it was used for making cookware and weapons. By around 1100 AD, it was being used to make pots in England. By the 15th century, it was used to make cannons.

When stovetops were invented in the 1700s and food no longer needed to be cooked outdoors over an open fire, cookware technology began to advance rapidly. Abraham Darby came up with a way to produce pots and kettles that were made from thinner cast-iron and were more suitable for use in homes rather than outdoors. Around this time, George Washington's mother even included her cast-iron skillet in her will.

By the 1800s cast-iron was widely used, giving rise to still-popular name brands such as Wagner, Griswold, and Lodge.

Lately, questions are arising regarding the effects of chemicals used in modern cookware. This has led to renewed interest and popularity for the cast-iron skillet.

The Benefits

Love to Last a Lifetime

The cast-iron skillet is known for its durability. Rust or scratches can be repaired. This is something that could last a lifetime, as long as you use it properly. It can even be handed down for the next generation to enjoy.

Naturally Non-Stick

You get a convenient non-stick surface without harmful chemicals, simply iron and oil.

Leaner Fare

With a naturally non-stick surface, you won't need as much oil or fat for cooking dishes in a cast-iron skillet. You'll be enjoying the leaner yet tastier fare.

From Stovetop to Oven

It's durable enough to be used over an open fire, on the stovetop, and in the oven. Just imagine everything you can whip up without changing skillets.

A Decorative Touch

The rustic and natural vintage look of the cast-iron skillet can add a more interesting and visually appealing touch to a table setting.

Iron Boost

Cooking in a cast-iron skillet can actually boost your iron intake, particularly if you use it to prepare acidic dishes like applesauce and pasta with tomato sauce. You get enough iron to meet your requirements without reaching toxic levels.

Ways You Can Cook
with a Cast-iron Skillet

Sear, Sauté, and Stir-Fry

With a well-seasoned cast-iron skillet, you can cook over high heat without any sticking. Unlike non-stick skillets, which can't be used over high heat, you can sear and brown foods well with a cast-iron skillet. After sautéing or stir-frying over the stovetop, you can immediately put it in the oven without having to change skillets.

Bake

Cast-iron retains and distributes heat evenly, and this is ideal for baking. Cakes baked in it have a noticeably rich, browned, good-textured crust. It can also serve as both the baking skillet and the serving dish.

Braise

Cast-iron maintains both high and low heat very well. This makes it able to keep the heat even and stable for simmering. It's ideal for cooking cuts of meat that need to be cooked gently for long periods to soften.

Fry

Unlike other skillets, which lose heat when food is added to hot oil, a cast-iron skillet can keep the heat constant. You get crispier exteriors and juicier interiors in fried food.

Seasoning a Cast-iron Skillet

Seasoning a cast-iron skillet has two basic purposes:

1. To build a protective layer or patina over the surface that will protect it from damage such as rusting.
2. To make the skillet naturally non-stick.

Most experienced cast-iron skillet users recommend seasoning both old and new skillets, even those that are "pre-seasoned."

Here are the steps:
Note: For new skillets, go straight to Step 3. Also, keep your kitchen well ventilated when seasoning your skillet, as this process can cause the oil to smoke and produce an unpleasant odor.

1. Preheat the oven to 350°F (177°C).
2. Wash the whole skillet, including the handle and outer surface, with warm, soapy water and a sponge. Do not use steel wool, as this may scratch the skillet and ruin it. Wash it thoroughly. It should be noted that this is the **only time** you use soapy water when cleaning cast-iron!
3. Rinse the skillet with hot water and wipe it dry.
4. Place the skillet in the hot oven to dry. It should be completely dry. (You may also let it dry on the stovetop; just make sure that all moisture evaporates.)
5. Dip a paper towel in vegetable oil. Flaxseed oil is best, but you can use others like canola oil or coconut oil; you can even use lard.
6. Rub the oiled paper towel over the cast-iron skillet to make a thick, even coat. You should cover both the inside and outside of the skillet. Use a clean, dry paper towel to remove any excess oil. Too much oil will leave the skillet too sticky.
7. Place the cast-iron skillet in the preheated oven, upside down, and in the center. Place a baking sheet or aluminum foil underneath to catch any drips.
8. Bake for exactly an hour.
9. Turn off the oven, but leave the cast-iron skillet inside.
10. Allow it to cool completely. Cast-iron retains heat, so this will take time.
11. Wipe away any excess oil to leave a smooth, shiny skillet. You don't want puddles of oil in your skillet.

And that is all you need to do. You can repeat the process whenever your skillet looks rusted or dull. General cooking, especially when using oil, will often keep the skillet seasoned.

Taking Care of Your Skillet

Seasoning twice a year is the best way to maintain your cast-iron skillet. It will keep your skillet in tip-top shape and help it last for a long time.

After use, immediately rinse the skillet by running hot water over it and wiping it to clean. To remove bits of stuck-on food, use a non-metal brush and scrub with coarse salt. This will help remove the food without wrecking the skillet. Sometimes, all you'll need is to wipe it clean using oil.

To avoid rust, always keep the skillet dry. After washing, dry the skillet thoroughly. Drying with a towel is usually adequate, but if you live in an especially humid environment, dry it in the oven or let the moisture in the skillet evaporate fully by heating over a stovetop. Leaving a cast-iron skillet wet will cause rust to form, and this will shorten the life of your skillet. If rust does form, use steel wool to remove it, but do not apply the steel wool to non-rusted parts of the skillet. After removing the rust, season the skillet again.

Finally, spray your skillet with a small amount of cooking oil after each time you wash it. Place a paper towel inside the skillet and store.

Proper care and maintenance of your cast-iron skillet will pay off as you will enjoy many years of using it. This means a lot of savings as well!

Other Helpful Pointers

Prepare in Advance

A cast-iron skillet retains heat so efficiently that you'll find the ingredients cooking more quickly than they would in an ordinary skillet. It's best to have everything ready so you can take advantage of the retained heat and avoid burning because you were busy chopping the next ingredient.

Preheat Your Skillet

Cast-iron skillets are great at retaining heat, but they can take a bit longer to heat up. There is, however, still some debate as to whether it's better to heat the skillet before adding oil or to heat the skillet along with the oil. Be extra careful when preheating on an electric range, as the heating coils may not heat up evenly and this could warp your skillet. Use medium-low to medium heat to preheat.

Choose the Skillet You'll Need

For beginners, don't go buying a whole set in one go. The recipes here call for either a 10- or 12-inch skillet. As the cast-iron skillet absorbs aromas and flavors, you may eventually want to have one for savory dishes and another one for desserts.

Keep Safe

Always use oven mitts; the skillet's handles will be as hot as the skillet itself! Have other tools like tongs on hand to keep yourself safe from burns.

An additional warning: Because a cast-iron skillet can heat up to a very high temperature, it could crack if cold water is suddenly added to it.

Choose the Right Oil

Although popular cooking oils are fine to use, remember that the skillet can take temperatures beyond the smoking point of many oils. Here are some oils that have high smoking points and will not degrade or produce smoke at high heat.

- Grape seed oil
- Peanut oil
- Palm oil
- Avocado oil

Keep Food in Containers

Leaving acidic ingredients like tomato sauce in a cast-iron skillet will cause too much iron to leach out and blacken your food. Remove acidic food immediately after cooking and transfer it to a storage container.

Experiment and Create Your Own Recipes

As you try out the following recipes, you'll become familiar with the basic procedures for preparing different dishes. Don't hesitate to try out your own ingredients and create your own recipes. You can start out by simply using your own substitutes for some of the ingredients. Very soon, you'll be able to develop your own techniques and secrets to using your cast-iron skillet.

Measuring Temperature
in Campfire Cooking

Since you're going to find yourself cooking outdoors without your usual kitchen equipment, it may be a challenge to know exactly the campfire's cooking temperature. But worry not as there's a simple way for you to get a rough estimate of a fire's temperature when campfire cooking and it's called the "hand test."
To do this test, all you have to do is hover your hand just above the cooking area (about 12 inches). The duration you're able to hold out your hand over the heat will give you an estimate of the fire's temperature.
<1 second: 600°F or 316°C (high)
1-2 seconds: 400-500°F or 204-260°C (medium-high)
3-4 seconds: 350-375°F or 177-191°C (medium)
5-7 seconds: 325-350°F or 163-177°C (low)

That's it. **Please be careful not to burn your hand when doing this test**.

Food Safety Reminders

I would not feel comfortable without any words on food safety and this is especially true when you are on the road or at the campsite.

When cooking outdoors, it is important to be diligent when it comes to food safety. Whether you have a portable refrigerator in your camper or you are depending upon your trusty cooler and ice or ice packs, keeping perishable foods at a temperature of 40°F or lower is priority number one. It takes barely any time at all for food-borne bacteria to invade your perishables.

It is a good idea to bring along, at least one, if not several food thermometers to monitor the temperature of foods both during refrigeration and during cooking. Also, never leave cooked food sitting out too long. Once you are finished eating, any leftovers should be properly packaged and refrigerated. Always thoroughly wash any working surface where raw ingredients have been resting or worked on including cutting boards and tools.

When handling, cooking, and storing food, safe steps need to be taken and shouldn't be taken likely. It's important to observe food safety measures as it helps prevent the spread of foodborne illnesses. Harmful bacteria cannot be detected through sight, smell, or taste. That's why with every step of food preparation, these four rules must be followed:

- **Clean**—Disinfecting of hands and surfaces often.
- **Separate**—Do not store raw meat with other foods.
- **Cook**—Cook to the right temperature.
- **Chill**—Do not delay food refrigeration.

Make sure that you cook your food to these minimum internal temperatures as measured with a food thermometer before removing food from the heat source.

If desired, consumers may choose to cook food to higher temperatures.

Product	Minimum Internal Temperature and Rest Time
Beef, Pork, Veal & Lamb Steaks, chops, roasts	145°F (62.8 °C) and allow to rest for at least 3 minutes
Ground Meats	160°F (71.1 °C)
Ground Poultry	165°F (73.9 °C)
Ham, fresh or smoked (uncooked)	145°F (62.8 °C) and allow to rest for at least 3 minutes
Fully-Cooked Ham (to be reheated)	Reheat cooked hams packaged in USDA-inspected plants to 140°F (60°C) and all others to 165°F (73.9°C).
All Poultry (breast, whole, leg, thigh, wing, ground, giblet, and stuffing)	165°F (73.9°C)
Eggs	160°F (71.1°C)
Fish and Shellfish	145°F (62.8°C)
Leftovers	165°F (73.9°C)
Casseroles	165°F (73.9°C)

Source: Food Safety and Inspection Service, USDA

So now that you know the tips; grab your cast-iron skillets and let's get started on the recipes!

BREAKFAST

Ham Omelet

A ham omelet is a fluffy omelet served with ham. It tastes delicious and makes a perfect campfire recipe. It is seasoned with salt, pepper, and chives. The melted cheese in the omelet tastes amazing.

Serves 4 | Prep. time 10 minutes | Cooking time 15 minutes

Ingredients
2 teaspoons vegetable oil
4 slices deli ham, chopped
4 eggs
2 teaspoons chopped chives
Slt and pepper to taste
½ cup shredded cheddar cheese, more for serving

Directions
1. Place the oil in a cast-iron skillet on hot coals or campfire over medium heat. If you don't have a thermometer, simply do the

hand test (page 9) to get an approximation of the fire's cooking temperature.
2. Add the ham and cook for 5-7 minutes until lightly golden. Transfer ham to a plate.
3. Beat the eggs with chives, salt, and pepper.
4. Pour the batter into the skillet and cook the omelet until the edges solidify.
5. Sprinkle the cheese on top, add the ham and fold the omelet in half. Let cook for 1-2 minutes until the cheese melt and serve with a sprinkle of cheese on top if desired..

Nutrition (per serving)
Calories 531, fat 38 g, carbs 6 g, sugar 0.9 g,
Protein 38 g, sodium 2379 mg

Blueberry Banana Pancake

Blueberry banana pancake is a classy recipe made with pancake batter, bananas, and blueberries. It's a fluffy and warm pancake perfect to start your morning.

Serves 6 | Prep. time 10 minutes | Cooking time 25 minutes

Ingredients
1 cup flour
⅓ cup powdered milk + 1 cup water, or 1 cup milk
2 tablespoons sugar
1 teaspoon baking powder
¼ teaspoon salt
1 egg
1 banana, sliced
½ cup blueberries
6 teaspoons butter
Maple syrup for serving

Directions
1. In a bowl, mix the powdered milk, sugar, salt, and flour. Add the water and eggs and whisk well.

2.   Heat a cast-iron skillet on the campfire over low heat. If you don't
      have a thermometer, simply do the hand test (page 9) to know
      approximatively the fire's cooking temperature.
3.   Add the butter and swirl to coat the skillet evenly.
4.   Pour in ⅓ cup of batter. Scatter some banana slices and
      blueberries over it.
5.   Cook for 2–3 minutes on each side.
6.   Serve with maple syrup.

Nutrition (per serving)
Calories 75, fat 0.7 g, carbs 12 g, sugar 2.5 g,
Protein 6.4 g, sodium 130 mg

Chocolate Granola

A yummy, healthy, and crunchy chocolate granola recipe you can have for breakfast or snack.

Serves 2 | Prep. time 2 minutes | Cooking time 10 minutes

Ingredients
1 cup rolled oats
¼ cup chopped almonds
¼ cup flaxseed
2 tablespoons chia seeds
2 teaspoons cocoa powder
1 tablespoon honey
2 tablespoons sugar
2 tablespoons olive oil
Pinch of salt

Directions
1. Heat a cast-iron skillet over hot coals or campfire on medium heat. If you don't have a thermometer, simply do the hand test (page 9) to get an approximation of the fire's cooking temperature.

2. Add the flaxseed and roast it well, then transfer it to a plate and set aside.
3. Add the chopped almonds to the skillet and roast for 1 minute. Transfer to the plate with the flaxseed.
4. Add the rolled oats to the skillet and roast them, then transfer to the same plate.
5. Add the coconut oil and honey to the skillet. Whisk well.
6. Add the cocoa powder, sugar, and salt and whisk well.
7. Mix in the roasted flaxseed, almonds, and oats.
8. Cook for 1 minute, then remove from heat and transfer to the plate.
9. Spread the mixture out and sprinkle the chia seeds over it.
10. Let cool, then break into clusters.

Nutrition (per serving)
Calories 450, fat 8 g, carbs 65 g, sugar 15 g,
Protein 5.6 g, sodium 400 mg

Camping Doughnuts

Camping doughnuts are a perfect treat early in the morning. These deep-fried doughnuts are simply made with biscuit dough and sprinkled with cinnamon sugar.

Serves 4 | Prep. time 10 minutes | Cooking time 4 minutes

Ingredients
Cinnamon sugar
½ cup sugar
½–1 tablespoon cinnamon

Other ingredients
½ can biscuit dough
½–1 cup vegetable oil for frying

Directions
1. Combine the cinnamon and sugar in a plastic resealable bag like a Ziploc before leaving for camping.

2. Heat the oil in a cast-iron skillet over medium-high heat. If you don't have a thermometer, simply do the hand test (page 9) to get an approximation of the fire's cooking temperature.
3. Cut the biscuit dough into four equal parts.
4. Place the doughnuts in the hot oil and cook for 15 seconds on each side. Remove when golden brown on both sides.
5. Place on a paper towel and sprinkle with the cinnamon-sugar mix.

Nutrition (per serving)
Calories 259, carbs 40 g, sugar 26 g,
Protein 2 g, sodium 255 mg

Huevos Rancheros with Beef

Very quick and easy to make, huevos rancheros with beef is a delicious dish for camping. This recipe is amazing for breakfast with flour tortillas dripping with beef, cheese, and egg for you to drool over.

Serves 4 | Prep. time 15 minutes | Cooking time 20 minutes

Ingredients
1 pound lean ground beef
1 small onion, chopped
2 (14½-ounce) cans diced tomatoes
1 cup frozen corn
4 ounces chopped green chilies
½ teaspoon salt
4 large eggs
¼ teaspoon pepper
6 tablespoons shredded cheddar cheese
6 flour tortillas, warmed

Directions
1. Cook the beef and onion in a cast-iron skillet over hot coals or campfire over medium heat for around 10 minutes. If you don't have a thermometer, simply do the hand test (page 9) to get an approximation of the fire's cooking temperature.
2. Crumble the beef and stir in the tomatoes, corn, chilies, and salt. Simmer.
3. Make four wells in the beef mixture and add an egg to each.
4. Season with salt and pepper. Cover and cook for 7 minutes.
5. Sprinkle with cheddar cheese.
6. Add the mixture to the tortillas and fold them before serving.

Nutrition (per serving)
Calories 434, fat 17 g, carbs 41 g, sugar 6 g,
Protein 29 g, sodium 879 mg

Sweet Potato with Egg Hash

Sweet potato with egg hash is an easy skillet recipe for a wholesome breakfast or even a nice supper. It's hearty and nourishing.

Serves 2-4 | Prep. time 15 minutes | Cooking time 30 minutes

Ingredients
½ tablespoon vegetable oil
4 slices bacon, cut into ½-inch thick pieces
1 small onion, diced
1 bell pepper, any color, diced
1 sweet potato, peeled and diced
¼ teaspoon cumin
¼ teaspoon garlic powder
¼ teaspoon paprika
Salt and pepper to taste
4 eggs

Directions
1. Heat the oil in a cast-iron skillet over medium heat. To gauge the campfire's cooking temperature, simply do the hand test (page 9).

2. Cook the bacon until golden brown, then remove it from the skillet to a plate lined with a kitchen paper towel to drain excess fat.
3. Sauté the onions and bell peppers for 2 minutes.
4. Add the sweet potato and all the spices and cook, covered with lid or foil for 10–15 minutes.
5. Cover and cook for 5 minutes more.
6. Add the bacon and cook for 2 minutes.
7. Create 4 wells in the hash and break the eggs into them. Cook until done.

Nutrition (per serving)
Calories 222, fat 13 g, carbs 15 g, sugar 9.4 g,
Protein 11 g, sodium 242 mg

French Toasts

Make exceptional French toast with this simple recipe during your next camping trip with the family.

Serves 12 | Prep. time 10 minutes | Cooking time 20 minutes

Ingredients
1 country loaf bread
6 large eggs, beaten
1 cup milk
2 tablespoons sugar
1 teaspoon cinnamon
1 teaspoon vanilla extract
Butter for frying and more for serving
Maple syrup, for serving

Directions
1. Slice the loaf into ¾ to 1-inch-thick slices.
2. In a bowl, mix eggs, milk, cinnamon, vanilla, and sugar.
3. Heat the butter in a cast-iron skillet over hot coals or campfire stove over medium heat. To gauge the campfire's cooking temperature, simply do the hand toast (page 9).

4. Dip each bread slice in the egg mixture and soak for 5-10 seconds on each side. Allow the excess to drip off before frying in the skillet.
5. Cook for about 2-3 minutes per side or until it's golden.
6. Repeat until all slices are cooked.
7. Serve with maple syrup and butter, if desired.

Nutrition (per serving)
Calories 148, fat 5 g, carbs 20 g, sugar 1 g,
Protein 6 g, sodium 142 mg

Bacon and Potato Hash

Bacon and potato hash are a yummy recipe with crispy bacon pieces, shallots, pepper, and potatoes seasoned with salt and pepper and thyme leaves.

Serves 4 | Prep. time 15 minutes | Cooking time 25 minutes

Ingredients
½ pound thick-cut bacon
2 tablespoons reserved bacon fat
1 tablespoon butter
2 small shallots, diced
½ green bell pepper, diced
2 potatoes, peeled and cut lengthwise
4 large eggs
Salt and pepper to taste

Directions
1. Cook the bacon in a cast-iron skillet over hot coals or campfire stove over medium heat. To gauge the campfire's cooking temperature, simply do the hand test (page 9).
2. Reserve the fat and set the bacon aside.

3. In another pot, boil the potatoes for 10 minutes. Cut them into ½-inch cubes.
4. In the cast-iron skillet, reheat the bacon fat with butter.
5. Fry the shallots for 4-5 minutes until tender, then add green pepper and cook for 2-3 minutes more.
6. Add the diced potatoes and season with salt and pepper to taste. Cook for 5 minutes.
7. Crumble the bacon and add to the potato hash and toss well.
8. Crack the eggs on top and let cook until the eggs are cooked, about 4-5 minutes.
9. Serve warm

Nutrition (per serving)
Calories 454, fat 17 g, carbs 25 g, sugar 3 g,
Protein 4 g, sodium 1148 mg

Egg Burritos

Egg burritos are tummy-filling and stuffed with eggs, cheese, shallot, and tomato. It's a scrumptious burrito to start the day.

Serves 4 | Prep. time 10 minutes | Cooking time 20 minutes

Ingredients
1 tablespoon butter
6 large eggs
½ teaspoon salt
¼ teaspoon pepper
4 (8-inch) tortillas
1½ cups shredded cheddar cheese
1 tomato, seeded and diced
1 small shallot, thinly diced

Directions
1. In a bowl, mix the eggs, salt, and pepper. Heat the cast-iron skillet over medium heat and melt the butter. To gauge the campfire's cooking temperature, simply do the hand test (page 9).
2. Scramble the egg mixture until cooked to your liking.
3. Spoon about ¼ cup of egg mixture onto each tortilla.

4. Sprinkle with cheese, tomato, and diced shallot.
5. Roll into burritos and serve.

Nutrition (per serving)
Calories 376, fat 20 g, carbs 29 g, sugar 2 g
Protein 19 g, sodium 726 mg

Grilled Cheese Sandwich

A grilled cheese sandwich is a crispy and cheesy sandwich. Toasted outside and gooey inside, it makes for one delicious morning.

Serves 1 | Prep. time 10 minutes | Cooking time 5 minutes

Ingredients
2 slices loaf bread
1 tablespoon butter
¼ cup grated cheddar cheese

Directions
1. Melt the butter in a cast-iron skillet over hot coals or campfire on medium-low heat. If you don't have a thermometer, simply do the hand test (page 9) to get an approximation of the fire's cooking temperature.
2. Spread the melted butter on the bread slices. Pile the cheese on the bread. Cover the bread with the skillet lid.
3. Cook for 2 minutes, flip, and cook for 2 minutes more.

Nutrition (per serving)
Calories 400, fat 6 g, carbs 39 g, sugar 6 g,
Protein 18 g, sodium 520 mg

Potato and Cheese Frittata

Another great and delicious breakfast is this potato and cheese frittata.

Serves 4 | Prep. time 15 minutes | Cooking time 25 minutes

Ingredients
2 tablespoons olive oil
2 large potatoes, peeled and shredded
1 onion, diced
4 eggs, beaten
½ cup grated Cheddar cheese
Salt and pepper to taste

Directions
1. Heat the oil in a cast-iron skillet over hot coals or campfire on medium heat. If you don't have a thermometer, simply do the hand test (page 9) to get an approximation of the fire's cooking temperature.
2. When hot, fry potatoes for about 15 minutes until it's crispy and golden.
3. Add onions and cook until softened.
4. Pour eggs and loosely cover the skillet with aluminum foil.
5. Cook until eggs are firm.
6. Carefully take off the foil and sprinkle the cheese. Cover it with the foil again.
7. Cook for another 3-5 minutes until the cheese has melted.

Nutrition (per serving)
Calories 354, fat 17 g, carbs 35 g, sugar 3 g,
Protein 14 g, sodium 286 mg

CHICKEN AND TURKEY

Chicken Tex-Mex Quesadillas

Chicken quesadillas are crispy, tasty, delicious lunch solutions. These are packed with a yummy chicken mixture and served with guacamole.

Serves 4 | Prep. time 15 minutes | Cooking time 10 minutes

Ingredients
4 teaspoons unsalted butter, divided
4 8-inch flour tortillas
3 cups grated Monterey Jack or a Mexican blend cheese
1 cup chopped cooked chicken breast
1 cup black beans, rinsed
2 teaspoons chili powder
1 ripe avocado
2 tablespoons lime juice
½ teaspoon garlic powder
¼ teaspoon salt

Directions

1. In a bowl, mix the chicken, black beans, and chili powder.
2. Heat your cast-iron pan over hot coals or campfire on medium-high heat. To gauge the campfire's cooking temperature, simply do the hand test (page 9).
3. Add half the butter.
4. Place a tortilla on the heated pan and sprinkle 2 tablespoons of cheese over half the tortilla and 2 tablespoonfuls of the chicken mixture over the cheese. Top with another 2 tablespoons of cheese and fold the bare half of the tortilla over the filling.
5. Cover the pan and let it cook for about 2 minutes or until the cheese has begun to melt. Flip the quesadilla and cook uncovered until both sides are lightly browned.
6. Repeat until all are cooked.
7. In a bowl, mash the avocado with lime juice, garlic powder, and salt. Put in a container to prevent browning.
8. Serve the quesadillas with the avocado mixture.

Nutrition (per serving)

Calories 460, fat 6 g, carbs 40 g, sugar 5 g,
Protein 30 g, sodium 705 mg

Ginger Orange Thighs

Ginger orange thighs are a sweet and sour recipe made in ketchup, orange marmalade, and soy sauce and seasoned with ginger and seasoned salt.

Serves 4 | Prep. time 20 minutes | Cooking time 10 minutes

Ingredients
16 whole chicken thighs
1 cup all-purpose flour
3 teaspoons seasoned salt
⅓ cup vegetable oil
2 cups orange marmalade
1 cup ketchup
½ cup soy sauce
¾ teaspoon ground ginger

Directions
1. In a bowl, combine flour and seasoned salt. Add the chicken wings and toss well.
2. Heat the oil in a cast-iron skillet over hot coals or campfire on medium heat. To gauge the campfire's cooking temperature, simply do the hand test (page 9).

3.   Add the chicken thighs, orange marmalade, ketchup, soy sauce, and ginger. Cook for 15 minutes.

Nutrition (per serving)
Calories 119, fat 5 g, carbs 14 g, sugar 2 g
Protein 6 g, sodium 399 mg

French Onion Chicken

French onion chicken is an old-fashioned lunch recipe made with onions, seasonings, and chicken breast. It tastes delicious mixed with some herbs and spices under a layer of cheese.

Serves 4 | Prep. time 10 minutes | Cooking time 35 minutes

Ingredients
3 tablespoons olive oil(divided)
1 large onion, thinly sliced
2 teaspoons chopped thyme
Salt and pepper to taste
2 cloves garlic, minced
1¾ pounds boneless skinless chicken breasts
2 tablespoons all-purpose flour
1½ cups chicken broth
1 cup shredded Gruyere cheese

Directions
1. Heat 2 tablespoons of olive oil in a cast-iron skillet over hot coals or campfire on medium heat. To gauge the campfire's cooking temperature, simply do the hand test (page 9).

2.   Add the onion and season with salt, pepper, and thyme. Cook
      for 25 minutes until the onion is caramelized.
3.   Add the garlic and cook for 1 minute. Remove the onion mixture
      from the skillet.
4.   In a bowl, season the chicken breast with salt and pepper.
5.   Heat the remaining 1 tablespoon of olive oil in the skillet. Add the
      chicken and cook for about 10 minutes until brown on all sides.
6.   Add the chicken broth and return the caramelized onion to the
      skillet. Cook for 10 minutes.
7.   Add the Gruyere cheese and close the lid. Wait for about 2
      minutes for the cheese to melt.

Nutrition (per serving)
Calories 289, fat 6.2 g, carbs 8.2 g, sugar 2 g,
Protein 48 g, sodium 451 mg

Lemon Chicken

Lemon chicken thighs is an easy family recipe that's great for camping. It is deliciously cooked chicken with flavors of garlic and lemon for a perfect blend.

Serves 4 | Prep. time 10 minutes | Cooking time 30 minutes

Ingredients
1 tablespoon olive oil
4 bone-in, skin-on chicken thighs
Salt and pepper to taste
2 tablespoons butter
3 cloves garlic, minced
Juice of 1 lemon
Lemon slices for garnishing

Directions
1. Heat the oil in a cast-iron skillet over hot coals or campfire stove on medium heat. To gauge the campfire's cooking temperature, simply do the hand test (page 9).
2. Add the chicken thighs, season with salt and pepper, and cook for 10 minutes. Transfer the chicken to a plate.

3.   In the skillet, mix together the butter, garlic, and lemon juice.
      Cook for 2 minutes.
4.   Return the chicken thighs to the skillet and cook for 5 minutes.
5.   Garnish with lemon slices before serving.

Nutrition (per serving)
Calories 180, fat 12 g, carbs 1 g, sugar 1 g
Protein 14 g, sodium 230 mg

Stuffed Chicken Breasts

Jalapeño popper chicken is a scrumptious recipe, full of taste and heavenly awesome looking! The stuffed chicken breast wrapped with bacon makes it a unique meal.

Serves 4 | Prep. time 10 minutes | Cooking time 30 minutes

Ingredients
8 ounces cream cheese or goat cheese, softened
⅓ cup sliced green onions
2 cloves garlic, minced
1 jalapeño, minced
Salt and pepper to taste
4 boneless skinless chicken breasts
12 slices bacon

Directions
1. In a bowl, mix together the cream cheese, garlic, and season with salt and pepper.

2. Make a pocket in each chicken breast and fill it with the cheese mixture. Wrap the chicken in the bacon slices. Secure with toothpick if needed.
3. Heat the oil in a cast-iron skillet over hot coals or campfire on medium heat. To gauge the campfire's cooking temperature, simply do the hand test (page 9).
4. Cook the bacon wrapped chicken for 10-15 minutes per side or until the internal temperature of the chicken reaches 165°F (74°C).

Nutrition (per serving)
Calories 520, fat 20 g, carbs 15 g, sugar 0 g
Protein 66 g, sodium 600 mg

Sesame Chicken Bites

Sesame chicken bites are a perfect camping appetizer recipe. These are crispy bites with a heavenly taste.

Serves 4 | Prep. time 10 minutes | Cooking time 15 minutes

Ingredients
½ cup dry breadcrumbs
¼ cup sesame seeds
1 teaspoon onion powder
1 teaspoon ground mustard
¼ teaspoon pepper
1 pound boneless skinless chicken breasts, cubed
2–4 tablespoons vegetable oil

Directions
1. In a bowl, mix the breadcrumbs and sesame seeds. In another bowl, mix the mayonnaise and seasonings.
2. Dip the chicken cubes in the mayonnaise mixture and then in the breadcrumb mixture to coat well.
3. In a cast-iron skillet, heat the oil over hot coals or campfire on medium heat. To gauge the campfire's cooking temperature, simply do the hand test (page 9).

4.   Add the chicken cubes and cook until no longer pink.

Nutrition (per serving)
Calories 102, fat 9 g, carbs 2 g, sugar 1 g,
Protein 4 g, sodium 73 mg

Turkey Burgers

Turkey burgers are the best recipe to make for lunch with minimum effort. Mix your patty mixture with ground turkey and season with Worcestershire sauce and other seasonings. Voila! Your hamburger is ready.

Serves 4 | Prep. time 10 minutes | Cooking time 20 minutes

Ingredients
1 pound ground turkey
1 large egg, beaten
2 cloves garlic, minced
1 tablespoon Worcestershire sauce
2 tablespoons freshly chopped parsley
Salt and pepper to taste
1 tablespoon vegetable oil, more if needed
4 hamburger buns
Mayonnaise as needed
4 lettuce leaves
4 tomato slices
4 cheese slices

Directions
1. In a large bowl, mix the turkey with the egg, garlic, Worcestershire sauce, and parsley. Season with salt and pepper. Form 4 patties.

2. Heat the oil in a cast-iron skillet over medium-high heat. To gauge the campfire's cooking temperature, simply do the hand test (page 9).
3. Cook the patties for 4-5 minutes until golden brown per side or until the internal temperature reaches 165°F (74°C).
4. Warm the hamburger buns, if desired, in same skillet.
5. Spread generously the buns with mayonnaise and add patties to the bottom buns. Top with cheese, tomato, and lettuce and serve.

Nutrition (per serving)
Calories 217, fat 12 g, carbs 40 g, sugar 0 g,
Protein 25 g, sodium 400 mg

Creamy Chicken Pasta

Serves 4 | Prep. time 10 minutes | Cooking time 30 minutes

Ingredients

1¼ pounds boneless skinless chicken breasts, cut into 1-inch pieces
3 tablespoons olive oil
2 cloves garlic, minced
1 cup heavy cream
1 (14-ounce) can low-sodium chicken broth
½ pound penne pasta (or any small pasta)
2 cups shredded Parmesan cheese, more for serving
Handful basil leaves
Salt and pepper

Directions

1. Season the chicken with ½ teaspoon salt and a few pinches of black pepper.
2. Add the oil to a large cast-iron skillet and heat it over medium-high heat. To gauge the campfire's cooking temperature, simply do the hand test (page 9).
3. Add the chicken and stir-cook until lightly browned.

4. Add the garlic and sauté while stirring until softened, about 1 minute.
5. Mix in the chicken broth, cream, and pasta.
6. Allow the pasta mixture to boil gradually. Turn down heat to low. Add the basil leaves.
7. Cover and allow the mixture to simmer for 15–20 minutes, until the pasta is cooked to your satisfaction. Season to taste with black pepper and salt.
8. Add the parmesan cheese. Stir to coat and continue cooking for 2-4 minutes.
9. Serve warm with the more Parmesan cheese.

Nutrition (per serving)
Calories 688, fat 31 g, carbs 47 g, sugar 0 g
Protein 44 g, sodium 849 mg

Pineapple Sweet and Sour Chicken

Serves 4 | Prep. time 10 minutes | Cooking time 12 minutes

Ingredients
1½ pounds skinless, boneless chicken thighs or breasts, cut into bite-sized pieces
2 tablespoons vegetable oil, more if needed
1 red bell pepper, cut into ¾-inch pieces
1 onion, chopped
1 (8-ounce) can pineapple tidbits with juice, drained
¾ cup sweet-and-sour sauce

Directions
1. Add the oil to a cast-iron skillet and heat it over medium-high heat. To gauge the campfire's cooking temperature, simply do the hand test (page 9).
2. Add the chicken; stir-cook for 5–6 minutes until no longer pink. Transfer to a plate and cover with foil to keep warm.
3. Add the onion and bell pepper and stir fry for 2-3 minutes. Add oil if needed.
4. Add the sauce and pineapple and continue to cook for about 4-5 minutes or until the pepper is tender sauce is warm.
5. Serve warm.

Nutrition (per serving)
Calories 420, fat 15 g, carbs 34 g, sugar 0 g
Protein 36 g, sodium 400 mg

Chicken Enchilada Pasta

Serves 6 | Prep. time 10 minutes | Cooking time 25–30 minutes

Ingredients
2 cloves garlic, minced
½ small onion, diced
2 tablespoons olive oil
1¼ pounds ground chicken
1 pack low-sodium taco seasoning
2 cups low-sodium chicken broth
2½ cups rotini pasta
1 (19-ounce) can red enchilada sauce
2 cups Colby Jack cheese, shredded

Directions
1. Add the oil to the cast-iron pot and heat it over medium-high heat. To gauge the campfire's cooking temperature, simply do the hand test (page 9).
2. Add the onions and garlic and sauté while stirring until softened, about 4 minutes.
3. Add the turkey and stir-cook until lightly browned. Break it up using a spatula.
4. Add the chicken broth, pasta and enchilada sauce.
5. Allow the pasta mixture to boil gradually.
6. Turn down heat to low. Cover and cook the mixture, stirring periodically, until the pasta is cooked to your satisfaction, about 15 minutes.
7. Remove cover and cook for 4–5 minutes more to thicken the sauce.
8. Take the pasta mixture off the heat and mix in the cheese until it melts completely.
9. Serve warm.

Nutrition (per serving)
Calories 682, fat 26 g, carbs 62 g, sugar 1 g,
Protein 41 g, sodium 1130 mg

Chicken Thighs
with Creamy Spinach Sauce

Tasty chicken thighs cooked with creamy tomato basil spinach sauce make a glorious meal that's ready in 30 minutes.

Serves 4 | Prep. time 10 minutes | Cooking time 20 minutes

Ingredients
1 tablespoon olive oil
1½ pounds boneless skinless chicken thighs
½ teaspoon salt
¼ teaspoon pepper
1 cup tomato sauce
2 cloves garlic, minced
½ cup heavy cream
4 ounces spinach
4 leaves basil
¼ cup grated Parmesan cheese

Directions
1. Season the chicken thighs with salt and pepper.
2. Heat the oil in a cast-iron skillet over hot coals or campfire on medium heat and add the chicken thighs. To gauge the campfire's cooking temperature, simply do the hand test (page 9).
3. Cook for 5 minutes then flip and cook for 5 minutes more.
4. Remove from the skillet and set aside.
5. In the same skillet, bring the tomato sauce, garlic, and heavy cream to boil.
6. Add the spinach and basil. Mix well.
7. Add the cooked chicken thighs and cook until done.

Nutrition (per serving)
Calories 533, fat 44 g, carbs 6 g, sugar 2 g,
Protein 32 g, sodium 852 mg

Cheesy Chicken Caprese

Skillet chicken Caprese is juicy, tender, and topped with mozzarella cheese. It is served with tomato, basil, and a glaze of balsamic vinegar.

Serves 4 | Prep. Time 10 minutes | Cooking time 20 minutes

Ingredients
8 boneless skinless chicken thighs or 4 breasts
1 tablespoon garlic butter, more if needed
2 tablespoons olive oil, more if needed
½ pound mozzarella cheese, cut into slices
2 medium tomatoes, sliced
Salt and pepper to taste

Directions
1. Pat the chicken with a paper towels and season with salt and pepper.
2. In a cast-iron skillet, heat the butter and olive oil over medium-low heat. To gauge the campfire's cooking temperature, simply do the hand test (page 9).
3. Add the chicken and cook it for 5 minutes and turn over and continue cooking for 3-4 minutes more or until the internal temperature reaches 165°F on an instant thermometer inserted in the thickest part of the chicken.
4. Top the chicken with tomato slices mozzarella slices. Cover with lid or foil and cook for 1-3 minutes or until the cheese has melted.
5. Serve warm.

Nutrition (per serving)
Calories 500, fat 65 g, carbs 98 g, sugar 52.4 g,
Protein 4.5 g, sodium 413 mg

BEEF AND PORK

Ground Beef Skewers

Ground beef skewers are quickly ready for dinner. Perfect for a summer BBQ with family and friends over the campfire!

Serves 4 | Prep. time 10 minutes | Cooking time 20 minutes

Ingredients
1 pound ground beef
2 tablespoons grated garlic
1½ tablespoons grated ginger
½ medium red onion, diced thin
1½ tablespoons vegetable oil

Directions
1. Mix all of the ingredients together in a bowl EXCEPT the oil.
2. Shape the meat mixture around the skewers and set aside for 20 minutes.

3. Heat the oil in a cast-iron skillet over medium-high heat. To gauge the campfire's cooking temperature, simply do the hand test (page 9).
4. Add skewers and fry, turning frequently for 8-10 minutes or until the meat browns on all sides and is cooked through.

Nutrition (per serving)
Calories 322, fat 24 g, carbs 7.8 g, sugar 0.1 g,
Protein 17 g, sodium 297 mg

Beef Mushroom Burgers

Easy and quick to make beef mushroom burgers with a splendid surprise of salad, patty, and seasonings inside. A perfect mouthwatering treat for camping.

Serves 4 | Prep. time 15 minutes | Cooking time 10 minutes

Ingredients
Patties
½ pound mushrooms
1 pound ground beef
3 tablespoons chopped chives
1 egg, beaten
Large handful of breadcrumbs
Salt and pepper to taste

Salad
1 red onion, sliced
2 beefsteak tomatoes
1 teaspoon Dijon mustard
1 teaspoon balsamic vinegar
1 tablespoon olive oil
Pinch of salt and pepper

<u>Serving</u>
4 buns
Honey mustard sauce
Sliced tomatoes

Directions
1. Dice the mushrooms and place them in a large bowl.
2. Add the beef, eggs, chives, and breadcrumbs. Season with salt and pepper.
3. Mix well and make 4 patties.
4. To make the salad, slice the tomatoes and dice the onions. Add the vinegar, mustard, and oil with a pinch of salt and pepper. Mix well. Leave for 10 minutes.
5. Heat the oil in a cast-iron skillet over medium-high heat. To gauge the campfire's cooking temperature, simply do the hand test (page 9).
6. Fry the patties for 5 minutes or until it's crispy and lightly browned on each side.
7. Warm the buns, if desired, in the same skillet
8. Spread the honey mustard sauce on the inside of each bun to taste. Add a patty to each bottom buns, top with tomato slice and salad. Serve warm.

Nutrition (per serving)
Calories 270, fat 23 g, carbs 26 g, sugar 0 g,
Protein 13.5 g, sodium 310 mg

Bacon Cheeseburger Balls

Bacon cheeseburger balls are scrumptious and have a flavorful filling inside. These are cheesy, delightful appetizers perfect for a romantic camping trip.

Serves 4-6 | Prep. time 10 minutes | Cooking time 20 minutes

Ingredients
1 large egg
1 packet onion soup mix
1 pound ground beef
2 tablespoons all-purpose flour
2 tablespoons milk
1 cup shredded cheddar cheese
4 bacon strips, cooked and crumbled

Coating
2 large eggs
1 cup breadcrumbs
¼ cup oil, for frying

Directions

1. In a large bowl, combine the egg and onion soup mix.
2. Crumble the beef over the mixture and mix together.
3. Divide into 18 portions.
4. In another bowl, combine the flour and milk until smooth. Add the cheese and bacon. Mix well.
5. Shape the cheese mixture into 18 balls. Shape one beef portion around each cheese ball.
6. Beat the eggs for coating in a bowl. Dip the meatballs in the eggs, then coat them with breadcrumbs.
7. Heat the oil in a cast-iron skillet over medium-high heat. To gauge the campfire's cooking temperature, simply do the hand test (page 9).
8. Cook the balls for about 12 minutes until crispy and golden brown and cooked through.

Nutrition (per serving)

Calories 198, fat 14 g, carbs 8 g, sugar 2 g,
Protein 10 g, sodium 137 mg

Taco Skillet

This taco skillet is a perfect mix of ground beef, seasonings, veggies, and melted cheese on the top! A spicy and fresh taco skillet recipe for your family!

Serves 4 | Prep. time 10 minutes | Cooking time 20 minutes

Ingredients
1 tablespoon oil
1 red bell pepper, chopped
½ cup diced onions
1 tablespoon chili powder
1 pound ground beef
2 diced tomatoes
1 ½-2 cups cheddar cheese
Salt and pepper to taste
Corn chips

Directions

1. Heat the oil in a cast-iron skillet over medium heat. To gauge the campfire's cooking temperature, simply do the hand test (page 9).
2. Cook the bell peppers and onions for 5 minutes, or until soft.
3. Season with salt, pepper, and chili powder.
4. Add the ground beef and cook for 5 minutes until no longer pink.
5. Add the diced tomatoes and cheddar cheese. Cook for 2–3 minutes or until the cheese melts.
6. Serve warm with corn chips.

Nutrition (per serving)

Calories 355, fat 17 g, carbs 25 g, sugar 23 g,
Protein 12 g, sodium 950 mg

Mediterranean Peach Pork Chops

Skillet balsamic peach chops with feta cheese and basil is a nutritious and healthy lunch recipe. It has seasoned pork chops served with peach slices and topped with feta cheese and basil to give a delicious and cheesy taste.

Serves 4 | Prep. time 10 minutes | Cooking time 15 minutes

Ingredients
4 bone-in pork chops
Salt and pepper to taste
2 tablespoons olive oil
½ cup balsamic vinegar
1 tablespoon honey
2 peaches, sliced
8 ounces feta cheese, crumbled
½ cup basil, sliced

Directions
1. Season the pork chops with salt and pepper.
2. Add the oil to a cast-iron skillet and cook the seasoned pork chops over medium-high heat for 5 minutes. To gauge the campfire's cooking temperature, simply do the hand test (page 9).
3. Reduce heat and cook the pork chops for 10 minutes more.
4. In a bowl, whisk together the balsamic vinegar, and honey. Add the sauce to the skillet.
5. Add the peach slices. Top with the feta cheese and basil.
6. Remove from heat and serve.

Nutrition (per serving)
Calories 392, fat 18 g, carbs 50.5 g, sugar 17.5g,
Protein 55g, sodium 240 mg

Pork Chops with Apples and Butternut Squash

Pork chops with apples and butternut squash is a delicious one pan meal. It is a simple recipe to make with butternut squash, rosemary, apple cider, and pork chops.

Serves 4 | Prep. time 10 minutes | Cooking time 30 minutes

Ingredients
4 thick-cut pork chops
Salt and pepper to taste
2 teaspoons Italian seasoning
¼ cup butter (divided), more if needed
3 cups butternut squash, cubed
1 small yellow onion, diced
5 cloves garlic, minced
1 teaspoon minced rosemary
2 tablespoons brown sugar
½ teaspoon ground cinnamon
¾ cup spiced apple cider
2 apples, cored, peeled, and sliced

Directions
1. Season the pork chops with salt, pepper, and Italian seasoning. Set aside.
2. Melt some of the butter in a cast-iron skillet. Cook the pork chops for 6-7 minutes over medium heat on each side until golden brown and cooked through. To gauge the campfire's cooking temperature, simply do the hand test (page 9).
3. Add more butter. Add the butternut squash and cook for 8 minutes. Add the onion and cook for 5-6 minutes until tender.
4. Add the minced garlic, rosemary, brown sugar, and cinnamon. Cook for 2 minutes.
5. Mix in the spiced apple cider and sliced apples and continue cooking for 4-5 minutes until apples are soft.
6. Return the pork chops to the skillet and continue cooking for 5 minutes.
7. Top the pork chops with butter and serve.

Nutrition (per serving)
Calories 463, fat 21 g, carbs 39 g, sugar 22 g,
Protein 30 g, sodium 175 mg

Potato, Cabbage, and Sausage Skillet

A one-pot dinner dish with a few ingredients. It's filling, healthy, hearty, and a great camping idea.

Serves 4 | Prep. time 10 minutes | Cooking time 20 minutes

Ingredients
1 small head cabbage, chopped
4 medium potatoes, chopped
4 sausages, chopped
Salt and pepper to taste
1 teaspoon garlic powder
1 cup water

Directions
1. Prepare the campfire or barbecue grill.
2. In a large cast-iron skillet, layer the chopped cabbage, potatoes, and sausages. Season with salt, pepper, and garlic powder.
3. Add the water, cover with lid or foil, and place over the campfire grill or barbecue grill over medium heat for 20 minutes or until the veggies are fork-tender and sausages are cooked through. If

coking over the campfire, to gauge the campfire's cooking temperature, simply do the hand test (page 9).
4. Serve warm.

Nutrition (per serving)
Calories 320, fat 8 g, carbs 22 g, sugar 2 g,
Protein 5 g, sodium 430 mg

Bacon Spinach Quiche

Quiche is something that mixes and matches any vegetables with eggs, meat, cheese, and seasonings to make a worthwhile dish.

Serves 4-6 | Prep. time 10 minutes | Cooking time 20 minutes

Ingredients
1 prepared crust 10-inch (optional)
8 eggs
1 ½ to 2 cups baby spinach, chopped
1 pound bacon
10-12 cherry tomatoes, cut into half
1 cup shredded cheese, plus more for topping
Salt and pepper to taste

Directions
1. Prepare the campfire or barbecue grill and set it to have medium heat. To gauge the campfire's cooking temperature, simply do the hand test (page 9).
2. Stir-fry the bacon in a cast-iron skillet and transfer to a plate lined with paper towels. Crumble the bacon and set it aside.
3. Remove skillet from heat, leave about 1 tablespoon of bacon grease in the skillet.

4.   If using, spread the prepared crust at the bottom of the skillet.
5.   Whisk the eggs in a bowl.
6.   Add the chopped spinach, bacon, cherry tomatoes, and shredded cheese to the eggs. Season with salt and pepper to taste and whisk to combine.
7.   Pour the mixture into the skillet and cook, covered with lid or foil, for 20 minutes or until the eggs are set and cooked through. Uncover and add some cheese on top. Continue cooking for 10 minutes for the cheese to melt. Remove from heat.
8.   Let rest 10 minutes before slicing.

Nutrition (per serving)
Calories 208, fat 14 g, carbs 11 g, sugar 3g,
Protein 9 g, sodium 338 mg

Italian Sausage Pasta Skillet

This Italian sausage skillet will satisfy any hungry campers.

Serves 4 | Prep. Time 10 minutes | Cooking time 10 minutes

Ingredients
1 pound fettuccine pasta, cooked according to package directions
1 pound Italian sausages, hot or mild, casings removed
1 medium onion, chopped
1 garlic clove, minced
2 (14-ounce) cans diced tomatoes
Salt and pepper to taste
Parmesan for serving

Directions
1. Heat the oil in a cast-iron skillet over medium heat. To gauge the campfire's cooking temperature, simply do the hand test (page 9).
2. Break up the sausages and cook with onion for 6-8 minutes until the sausages are no longer pink.
3. Add the garlic and cook for 1 minute.
4. Add the tomatoes, salt, and pepper and cook for 2–3 minutes.

5.   Add the cooked pasta before serving.
6.   Serve with parmesan cheese if desired.

Nutrition (per serving)
Calories 251, fat 6 g, carbs 35g, sugar 2 g
Protein 16 g, sodium 417 mg

Smoked Sausage and Spinach Pasta Skillet

Serves 4 | Prep. time 10 minutes | Cooking time 30 minutes

Ingredients
¾ pound dry linguine or other favorite dry pasta
2 tablespoons vegetable oil, divided
½ pound smoked sausages such as kielbasa, sliced
1 bunch fresh spinach
Salt and black pepper to taste
Grated Parmesan cheese for serving

Directions
1. Cook the pasta according to package directions less 1 minute. Drain the water add 1 tablespoon olive oil, stir to coat, and set aside.
2. In a large cast-iron skillet, warm the remaining oil and cook the sausages over medium heat until cooked through, about 8-10 minutes, taking care of turning over a few times.
3. Add the spinach and pasta and stir fry until spinach is welted, about 2-3 minutes.
4. Season with salt and pepper to taste.
5. Serve warm with grated Parmesan on the side.

Nutrition (per serving)
Calories 512, fat 27 g, carbs 23 g, sugar 0 g,
Protein 37 g, sodium 1456 mg

Campfire Pizza

Melted, gooey mozzarella, tasty pepperoni, and green peppers make this cast-iron pizza a favorite of all ages.

Serves 4 | Preparation time 10 minutes | Cooking time 20 minutes

Ingredients
1 (14-ounce) package pizza crust dough
Non-stick cooking spray
Jarred pizza sauce
1 (9-ounce) package pepperoni, sliced
½ green bell pepper trimmed and cut into thin strips
2-2½ cups shredded mozzarella cheese

Preparation
1. Grease a 12-inch cast-iron skillet with cooking spray.
2. Roll out pizza dough and place it in the skillet's bottom.
3. Cook the dough over a medium heat camp stove or campfire until the crust has a golden color at the bottom.

4. Turn the crust over and spread the pizza sauce over the crispy dough. Arrange the pepperoni and pepper strips on top and cover with the mozzarella cheese. Add a few pepperoni slices over the cheese.
5. Place onto the grill over the campfire or camp stove and cook until the cheese is melted, about 10 minutes.
6. Remove from heat. Let rest a few minutes before slicing.

Nutrition (per serving)
Calories 730, fat 49 g, carbs 36 g,
Protein 36 g, sodium 2361 mg

One-Pot Beefy Macaroni

Serves 4-6 | Prep. time 10 minutes | Cooking time 20 minutes

Ingredients
½ onion, chopped
1 pound ground beef
2 teaspoons Italian seasoning
2 cups hot water
1 (15-ounce) can tomato saucer
1 pound package dry macaroni pasta
Salt and pepper to taste
Grated Parmesan cheese for serving

Directions
1. On a large cast-iron skillet, add the onion and beef and stir-cook over medium-high heat until lightly browned, about 5–7 minutes. To gauge the campfire's cooking temperature, simply do the hand test (page 9).
2. Break the beef into small pieces.
3. If needed, remove the excess cooking grease and liquid and stir in Italian seasoning.
4. Add the water and pasta.

5.   Simmer the mixture, uncovered, stirring periodically, until the pasta is cooked, about 10–15 minutes and water has evaporated.

6.   Season with salt and pepper to taste. Serve warm with grated Parmesan cheese.

Nutrition (per serving)
Calories 350, fat 11.5 g, carbs 41 g, sugar 0 g,
Protein 21 g, sodium 445 mg

Bacon and Blue Cheese Pasta

Serves 4 | Prep. time 10 minutes | Cooking time 15 minutes

Ingredients
4 strips bacon, preferably thick cut
½ pound pasta
2 cups water or broth
2 cloves garlic, minced
⅓ cup crumbled blue cheese
¼ cup chopped sundried tomatoes
2 tablespoons milk or cream

Directions
1. On a large cast-iron skillet, add the bacon and cook over medium heat until crispy. To gauge the campfire's cooking temperature, simply do the hand test (page 9).
2. Set aside half the cooked bacon, drain on paper towels, and crumble.
3. Break the remaining bacon into chunks; stir in the pasta, water or broth, garlic, and tomatoes.
4. Cover and boil the mixture. Allow the mixture to simmer for 7–8 minutes, until the pasta is cooked and most of the water has evaporated.
5. Mix in the milk and cheese. Combine until the cheese melts and remove from the heat.
6. Serve hot and enjoy.

Nutrition (per serving)
Calories 504, fat 9 g, carbs 64 g, sugar 0 g,
Protein 22 g, sodium 274 mg

Bacon, Beef, and Beans Casserole

Bacon, beef, and beans casserole is a filling, heavy dinner with a tasty and crunchy texture for cold evenings.

Serves 4 | Prep. time 10 minutes | Cooking time 20 minutes

Ingredients
¾ pound bacon
¾ pound ground beef
1 (20-ounce) can baked beans
½ cup steak sauce
1 can biscuits

Directions
1. Heat the oil in a cast-iron skillet over medium heat. To gauge the campfire's cooking temperature, simply do the hand test (page 9).
2. Add the bacon and stir fry until crispy.
3. Mix in the ground beef, baked beans, and sauce. Keep stirring until it comes to a boil.
4. Lay the biscuits on top of the mixture, cover, and cook for 10 minutes more.

Nutrition (per serving)
Calories 223, fat 8 g, carbs 25 g, sugar 5 g,
Protein 11 g, sodium 471 mg

Glazed Smoked Sausages

Apricot slices are easy to make appetizer bites with a thick and zesty sauce and the right amount of sweetness.

Serves 4-6 | Prep. time 10 minutes | Cooking time 10 minutes

Ingredients
1 pound fully cooked smoked sausages such as Hunter or kielbasa sausages, sliced
1½ cups apricot preserves
2 tablespoons lemon juice
2 teaspoons Dijon mustard
¼ teaspoon ground ginger

Directions
1. Brown the sausages in a cast-iron skillet over medium heat, then remove them from the skillet to a plate. To gauge the campfire's cooking temperature, simply do the hand test (page 9).
2. Add the apricot preserves, lemon juice, Dijon mustard, and ground ginger to the skillet. Stir-cook for 2–3 minutes.
3. Mix in the sausages before serving.

Nutrition (per serving)
Calories 154, fat 13 g, carbs 5 g, sugar 4 g,
Protein 6 g, sodium 110 mg

FISH AND SHRIMP

Poached Salmon
in Coconut Lime Sauce

Poached salmon is simple, exotic, and amazing with coconut lime sauce. It's also quick and easy to make. It has outstanding flavors of ginger, caramelized garlic, and lemongrass with sugar and coconut milk to give a good texture.

Serves 4 | Prep. time 10 minutes | Cooking time 35 minutes

Ingredients
4 salmon fillets
Salt and pepper
2 tablespoons oil
2 cloves garlic, grated
2 teaspoons grated ginger
1 tablespoon brown sugar
1 teaspoon chili garlic paste

1¾ cups coconut milk
1 tablespoon fish sauce
Juice of 2 limes
2 teaspoons lime zest
Coriander and hot chiles sliced for serving, if desired

Directions
1. Season both sides of the salmon with salt and pepper.
2. Heat the oil in the cast-iron skillet over medium-high heat. To gauge the campfire's cooking temperature, simply do the hand test (page 9).
3. Cook the salmon for 1 minute on each side. Transfer to a plate and set aside.
4. Heat the oil again in the same cast-iron skillet. Add the garlic and ginger. Cook for 1 minute.
5. Add the sugar and cook for 20 seconds to caramelize.
6. Stir in the garlic chili paste.
7. Mix in the coconut milk. Add the fish sauce, and lime juice, and cook for 5 minutes.
8. Place the salmon in the sauce and cook for 10-15 minutes.
9. Remove from the skillet and stir in lime zest.
10. Garnish with coriander and chiles if desired. Serve warm.

Nutrition (per serving)
Calories 502, fat 38 g, carbs 9 g, sugar 6 g,
Protein 32 g, sodium 435 mg

Cilantro Lime Shrimp

Cilantro lime shrimp is a healthy lunch recipe with butter, red peppers, and shrimp, and it's amazingly delicious.

Serves 2 | Prep. time 10 minutes | Cooking time 15 minutes

Ingredients
2–3 tablespoons butter
2–3 cloves garlic, chopped
1 pound shrimp, cleaned and deveined
Salt and pepper, to taste
2 tablespoons lime juice
1 tablespoon cilantro
½ teaspoon rosemary
8-10 baby tomatoes
Lime wedges for serving

Directions
1. Melt the butter in a cast-iron skillet over medium heat. To gauge the campfire's cooking temperature, simply do the hand test (page 9).
2. Sauté the garlic.
3. Add the shrimp and cook for 2 minutes.

4. Add tomatoes and season with salt and pepper to taste and stir in the rosemary. Continue cooking for 4-5 minutes.
5. Remove from heat. Stir in the lime juice.
6. Top with cilantro and serve with lime wedges.

Nutrition (per serving)
Calories 143, fat 9 g, carbs 2 g, sugar 1 g,
Protein 14 g, sodium 991 mg

Crispy Honey Walleye

Crispy honey walleye is a shallow fish fry side recipe with minimum effort. It's quick to make with an amazing egg and crackers coating.

Serves 4 | Prep. time 10 minutes | Cooking time 10 minutes

Ingredients
1 large egg
2 teaspoons honey
2 cups crushed Ritz crackers
½ teaspoon salt
1½ pounds walleye fillets
⅓–½ cup canola oil

Directions
1. In a bowl, beat the eggs with the honey. In another dish, combine the crackers and salt.
2. Dip the fish in the egg mixture and then in the cracker mixture to coat well.
7. Heat the oil in a cast-iron skillet over medium heat. To gauge the campfire's cooking temperature, simply do the hand test (page 9).

3. Cook the fillets for 5 minutes on each side until golden brown.
4. Serve warm.

Nutrition (per serving)
Calories 389, fat 22 g, carbs 23 g, sugar 5 g,
Protein 25 g, sodium 514 mg

Cajun Shrimp with Bell Peppers

Cajun shrimp with bell peppers, veggies, and Cajun spices makes a simple dinner that you can prepare in just 30 minutes.

Serves 4 | Prep. time 15 minutes | Cooking time 25 minutes

Ingredients
2 tablespoons oil (divided)
½ onion, chopped
2 bell peppers, chopped
2 teaspoons Cajun seasoning
1½ pounds shrimp, peeled
Salt and pepper to taste
1 tablespoon lime juice
Parsley for garnishing

Directions
1. Heat 1 tablespoon of oil in a cast-iron skillet over medium heat. To gauge the campfire's cooking temperature, simply do the hand test (page 9).
2. Sauté the onions and bell peppers for 5 minutes.
3. Add the garlic and cook for 1 minute. Transfer to the bowl.

4. Add the remaining oil to the skillet. Add shrimp in a single layer and season with salt and pepper and Cajun seasoning.
5. Cook for 1 minute.
6. Add the vegetables and lime juice and toss well.
7. Garnish with parsley before serving.

Nutrition (per serving)
Calories 103, fat 5 g, carbs 9 g, sugar 3 g,
Protein 7 g, sodium 224 mg

Soy Glazed Cod Fillets

Serves 4 | Prep. time 10 minutes | Cooking time 10 minutes

Ingredients
2 tablespoons fresh ginger, peeled and finely grated
3 tablespoons rice vinegar
2 tablespoons soy sauce
4 (6–8 ounce) skinless cod fillets
Coarse salt and ground pepper to taste
6 scallions (green parts), cut into 3-inch lengths

Directions
1. Season the fish evenly with ground black pepper and salt.
2. Add the rice vinegar, soy sauce, and ginger to a cast-iron skillet; heat it over medium-high heat. To gauge the campfire's cooking temperature, simply do the hand test (page 9).
3. Add the fish to the skillet and bring to a boil.
4. Cover and simmer over low heat for about 6–8 minutes until the fish is opaque.
5. Slice the chopped scallion greens lengthwise.

6. Add them to the skillet and combine well; stir-cook for about 2 minutes.
7. Serve warm.

Nutrition (per serving)
Calories 266, fat 2 g, carbs 14 g, sugar 0 g
Protein 41 g, sodium 643 mg

Spiced Sweet Tilapia

Serves 4 | Prep. time 10 minutes | Cooking time 5 minutes

Ingredients

¼ cup low-sodium soy sauce
3 tablespoons light brown sugar
1 pound tilapia fillets
1 teaspoon Chinese five-spice powder (or your choice of spice mix)
1 tablespoon canola oil
3 green onions, thinly sliced

Directions

1. Season the fillets evenly with the spice mix.
2. Combine the sugar and soy sauce in a mixing bowl until the sugar dissolves.
3. Add the oil to a cast-iron skillet and heat it over medium-high heat. To gauge the campfire's cooking temperature, simply do the hand test (page 9).
4. Add the fish fillets and stir-cook for about 2–3 minutes until opaque.
5. Reduce heat to medium, flip the fillets and add the soy sauce mixture on top.

6.   Bring to a boil, then simmer for about 2–3 minutes until the fish is easy to flake.
7.   Add the green onions and combine.
8.   Serve the fish warm.

Nutrition (per serving)
Calories 180, fat 6 g, carbs 9 g, sugar 0 g
Protein 24 g, sodium 596 mg

Prosciutto-Wrapped Cod Filet

Serves 4 | Prep. time 10 minutes | Cooking time 20 minutes

Ingredients
4 cod fillets
4 slices prosciutto ham
2 cups chicken stock
¼ cup sundried tomato, chopped
2 cloves garlic, grated
Salt and black pepper
Vegetable oil as needed

Directions
1. In a bowl, combine garlic, ½ teaspoon salt, ½ teaspoon black pepper, and mix.
2. Wrap each cod fillet with a prosciutto slice.
3. Heat 4 tablespoons vegetable oil in a cast-iron skillet over medium heat. To gauge the campfire's cooking temperature, simply do the hand test (page 9).
4. Add cod filets to skillet and cook 3 minutes per side.
5. Add sundried tomato and garlic mixture to skillet, and cook for 15 minutes.
6. Plate prosciutto-wrapped cod fillet with rice or zucchini noodles.

Nutrition (per serving)
Calories 300, fat 5 g, carbs 2 g, sugar 0 g,
Protein 59 g, sodium 611 mg

Pineapple Shrimp Stir Fry

Serves 4 | Prep. time 10 minutes | Cooking time 10 minutes

Ingredients:
1 pound shrimp, peeled and deveined
½ cup chopped pineapple
½ cup shallots, chopped
1 lemon, juiced
1 teaspoon salt
Extra virgin olive oil

Directions
1. Heat 3 tablespoons olive oil in a medium cast-iron skillet. To gauge the campfire's cooking temperature, simply do the hand test (page 9).
2. Add shallots and sauté for 2 minutes.
3. Add pineapple and sauté for 3-4 minutes or until caramelization begins to take place.
4. Sprinkle in salt. Add shrimp, sauté until pink, remove from heat.
5. Allow shrimp to sit in pineapple for a few minutes to soak in juices before serving.
6. Squeeze lemon juice over shrimp and serve with rice or noodles.

Nutrition (per serving)
Calories 300, fat 10 g, carbs 12 g, sugar 3 g
Protein 41 g, sodium 611 mg

VEGETARIAN

Creamy Fettuccine Alfredo

Fettuccine Alfredo is one of the most delicious and cheesiest pasta dinners. It's simple to make with seasonings and garnished with fresh parsley.

Serves 4 | Prep. time 10 minutes | Cooking time 30 minutes

Ingredients
1 pound fettuccine
½ cup heavy cream
½ cup butter
½ cup grated Parmesan
Salt and pepper to taste

Directions
1. Cook the fettuccine as per the package directions. Drain and set aside.
2. Heat the butter and heavy cream in a cast-iron skillet over medium heat until the cream is bubbling. To gauge the campfire's cooking temperature, simply do the hand test (page 9).

3. Add the salt and pepper and Parmesan cheese. Cook for 2 minutes.
4. Add the cooked pasta and toss well with the sauce.
5. Serve warm.

Nutrition (per serving)
Calories 668, fat 60 g, carbs 14 g, sugar 0.5 g,
Protein 5.9 g, sodium 377 mg

Vegetarian Campfire Nachos

Campfire nachos are a flaky, crispy, and tasty snack recipe cooked with three layers of chips, sauces, cheese, black beans, and onions!

Serves 2 | Prep. time 10 minutes | Cooking time 10 minutes

Ingredients
1 tablespoon oil
½ pound tortilla chips
1 cup tomato sauce
1 cup shredded Mexican cheese blend
1 (14½-ounce) can black beans, drained
4–5 green onions, sliced
Handful of cilantro, chopped (optional)

Directions
1. Grease a cast-iron skillet with oil.
2. For the first layer, spread ⅓ of the tortilla chips in the skillet. Top with ⅓ of the tomato sauce, black beans, cheese, and onions. Sprinkle with cilantro leaves, if desired.
3. Repeat the second and third layers in the same way.

4. Cover the skillet and cook over medium heat for 10 minutes. To gauge the campfire's cooking temperature, simply do the hand test (page 9).

Nutrition (per serving)
Calories 543, fat 15 g, sugar 4 g, carbs 33 g,
Protein 22 g, sodium 890 mg

Fried Cheese Ravioli

Fried ravioli are tasty and make a great appetizer to share or a meal served with a side salad. The ravioli are dipped in bread crumbs, all-purpose flour, and eggs and then deep-fried in a cast-iron skillet.

Serves 4 | Prep. time 10 minutes | Cooking time 20 minutes

Ingredients
1 cup dry breadcrumbs
2 teaspoons pepper
1½ teaspoons dried oregano
1 teaspoon salt
1 cup all-purpose flour
2 large eggs, lightly beaten
1 (19-ounce) frozen cheese ravioli, thawed
Vegetable oil for frying
Marinara sauce for serving

Directions
1. Mix the breadcrumbs and seasonings in a bowl. Place the eggs and flour in two separate bowls.
2. Dip the ravioli in the flour, then the egg, and then the breadcrumb mixture.

3. Heat the oil in a deep cast-iron skillet over medium-high heat To gauge the campfire's cooking temperature, simply do the hand test (page 9).
4. Fry the ravioli until golden brown, turning over after 1-2 minutes.
5. Drain on paper towels.
6. Serve with marinara sauce if desired.

Nutrition (per serving)
Calories 328, fat 14 g, carbs 38 g, sugar 3 g
Protein 13 g, sodium 440 mg

Asian Fried Rice

Asian fried rice is an easy-to-make meal for two. It is simply made with rice; soy sauce for a Chinese flavor; vegetables like peas, broccoli, onions, and cabbage; and eggs.

Serves 2 | Prep. time 20 minutes | Cooking time 20 minutes

Ingredients
1 ½ cups cooked rice (a day-old for best results)
2 tablespoons vegetable oil
1 pound frozen Asian vegetables mix
1 tablespoon soy sauce
2 small eggs, beaten
Salt and pepper

Directions
1. Heat the oil in a cast-iron skillet over medium heat. To gauge the campfire's cooking temperature, simply do the hand test (page 9).
2. Cook the chopped vegetables for 15 minutes.
3. Add the cooked rice and cook until it is slightly brown. Mix in the soy sauce.

4.   Mix in the beaten eggs and cook for 2–3 minutes.
5.   Taste and adjust seasoning with salt and pepper.

Nutrition (per serving)
Calories 268, fat 3g, carbs 48 g, sugar 1 g,
Protein 7 g, sodium 554 mg

Vegetarian Chili con Carne

This simple vegetarian chili makes for a hearty and delicious yet healthy meal.

Serves 4 | Prep. time 10 minutes | Cooking time 25 minutes

Ingredients
250 grams cooked red kidney beans, rinsed and drained
375 grams chopped tomatoes
250 grams vegetable stock
2 bell peppers, sliced
1 medium-sized carrot, peeled and sliced
1 medium-sized onion, peeled and sliced
1 celery stalk
2 garlic cloves, peeled and chopped
5 tablespoons tomato puree
1 tablespoon olive oil
½ tablespoon paprika
Salt and pepper to taste

Directions
1. Heat the olive oil in a cast-iron skillet over medium heat. To gauge the campfire's cooking temperature, simply do the hand test (page 9).
2. Add onion and garlic and sauté until they're soft.

3.   Add the tomato puree, tomatoes, and paprika. Cook for 2-3 minutes, stirring it occasionally.
4.   Add vegetable stock and stir well. Bring it to a boil.
5.   Once it boils, lower the heat and let it simmer for 2-3 minutes.
6.   Add in the carrot, celery, and bell peppers and simmer for 3-5 minutes. Then add the red kidney beans. Simmer until the beans are heated through.
7.   Serve hot with brown rice or baked sweet potato.

Nutrition (per serving)
Calories 94, fat 5 g, carbs 9 g, sugar 1 g,
Protein 1 g, sodium 1237 mg

Skillet Ratatouille

Skillet ratatouille is a healthy, nutritious, and crunchy veggie recipe. It's full of veggies like zucchini, eggplant, tomato, and onion. It tastes amazing with simple seasonings.

Serves 4 | Prep. time 15 minutes | Cooking time 40 minutes

Ingredients
2 tablespoons butter
2 teaspoons minced garlic
1 medium onion, diced
Salt and pepper to taste
1 tablespoon dry herb de Provence or Italian seasoning mix
2 tablespoons olive oil
2 medium zucchinis, sliced thin
1 Japanese eggplant, sliced thin
3 Roma tomato, sliced thin
1 small goat cheese log, crumbled
Salt and pepper to taste

Directions
1. Melt the butter in a deep 12-inch cast-iron skillet over medium-high heat. To gauge the campfire's cooking temperature, simply do the hand test (page 9).

2. Cook the onions for 3-4 minutes, until soft. Add garlic and Provence herbs can continue cooking for another 1-2 minutes. Season with salt and pepper to taste. Remove from heat and transfer the onion mixture to a plate.
3. Arrange the tomatoes, zucchinis, and eggplant slices in a spiral pattern to cover fully the skillet. Spread the onions mixture on top. Drizzle the olive oil over the veggies evenly. Cover with foil or lid. Place over the grill of the campfire. Let cook for 20-30 minutes, or until the veggies are soft.
4. Season with salt and pepper.
5. To serve, sprinkle some of the goat cheese on top.

Nutrition (per serving)
Calories 225, fat 8 g, carbs 35 g, sugar 3 g,
Protein 4 g, sodium 426 mg

Classic Skillet Corn

Serves 6 | Prep. time 5–10 minutes | Cooking time 15–20 minutes

Ingredients
3 cups corn, cut fresh from cobs
1 tablespoon sugar
¼ cup unsalted butter, melted
½ teaspoon salt
Ground black pepper to taste
½ cup water
1 tablespoon flour
¼ cup milk

Directions
1. Add the butter to a cast-iron skillet and melt it over medium-high heat. To gauge the campfire's cooking temperature, simply do the hand test (page 9).
2. Stir in the corn, water, salt, black pepper, and sugar.
3. Cover and simmer over medium heat for about 15 minutes.
4. Combine the milk and flour in a bowl; add the mixture to the skillet and combine well.
5. Stir-cook for 4–5 minutes. Serve warm.

Nutrition (per serving)
Calories 158, fat 9 g, carbs 19 g, sugar 0 g
Protein 3 g, sodium 267 mg

Parmesan Sweet Potato Ribbons

Serves 4 | Prep. time 5–10 minutes | Cooking time 15 minutes

Ingredients
¼ cup sage leaves, stemmed
¼ cup Parmesan cheese, grated
2 medium sweet potatoes
2 tablespoons unsalted butter, melted
Ground black pepper and salt to taste

Directions
1. Peel the potatoes, cut into thick slices, and then shave to make ribbons.
2. Add the butter to a cast-iron skillet and melt it over medium-high heat. To gauge the campfire's cooking temperature, simply do the hand test (page 9).
3. Add the sage leaves and stir-fry for 4–5 minutes until crispy.
4. Add the potato ribbons and stir-cook for 4–5 minutes until tender.
5. Season to taste with salt and pepper. Serve topped with Parmesan cheese.

Nutrition (per serving)
Calories 136, fat 7.5 g, carbs 14.5 g, sugar 0 g,
Protein 4 g, sodium 143 mg

Pesto Linguine Pasta

Serves 4 | Prep. time 10 minutes | Cooking time 20 minutes

Ingredients
1 pound green linguine or fettuccini, broken in half
2 tablespoons extra-virgin olive oil
4½ cups water
1 teaspoon kosher salt
1 cup grape tomatoes, halved
½ cup jarred pesto
Grated Parmesan for serving

Directions
1. Add the oil to a large skillet or saucepan and heat it over medium-high heat. To gauge the campfire's cooking temperature, simply do the hand test (page 9).
2. Add the pasta, salt, and water; allow the pasta mixture to boil.
3. Cook the mixture, stirring periodically until the pasta is cooked to your satisfaction, about 10 minutes. Drain the water, keep some of the cooking liquids.
4. Mix in the tomatoes and pesto. Add cooking liquid if the sauce is too thick and stir.

5.   Serve warm with some grated Parmesan cheese.

Nutrition (per serving)
Calories 298, fat 18 g, carbs 17 g, sugar 0 g
Protein 18 g, sodium 634 mg

Easy Mac and Cheese

Serves 6 | Prep. time 10 minutes | Cooking time 10–15 minutes

Ingredients
½ pound mild Cheddar, shredded
3 ounces mozzarella, shredded
1 quart whole milk
¾ pound elbow macaroni
2 tablespoons butter, melted
1 teaspoon Dijon mustard
Salt and black pepper to taste

Directions
1. On a large cast-iron skillet, add the macaroni and milk; heat over medium-high heat. To gauge the campfire's cooking temperature, simply do the hand test (page 9).
2. Cook the mixture, stirring a few times until the macaroni is tender and the mixture is thick, about 4–5 minutes.
3. Take it off the heat, mix in the mozzarella, Cheddar cheese, mustard, and butter. Season with salt and pepper to taste.
4. Serve warm.

Nutrition (per serving)
Calories 365, fat 22 g, carbs 29 g, sugar 0 g,
Protein 16 g, sodium 347 mg

Parmesan Sweet Potato Ribbons

Serves 4 | Prep. time 10 minutes | Cooking time 15 minutes

Ingredients
¼ cup sage leaves, stemmed
¼ cup Parmesan cheese, grated
2 medium sweet potatoes
2 tablespoons unsalted butter, melted
Ground black pepper and salt to taste

Directions
1. Peel the potatoes, cut into thick slices, and then shave to make ribbons.
2. Add the butter to a cast-iron skillet and melt it over medium-high heat. To gauge the campfire's cooking temperature, simply do the hand test (page 9).
3. Add the sage leaves and stir-fry for 4–5 minutes until crispy.
4. Add the potato ribbons and stir-cook for 4–5 minutes until tender.
5. Season to taste with salt and pepper. Serve topped with Parmesan cheese.

Nutrition (per serving)
Calories 136, fat 7.5 g, carbs 14.5 g, sugar 0 g
Protein 4 g, sodium 143 mg

SIDES

Flamed Veggies

Flamed veggies are easy to season with salt and pepper. Crunchy vegetables taste delicious and juicy.

Serves 2 | Prep. time 10 minutes | Cooking time 15 minutes

Ingredients
1 (12-ounce) package frozen vegetable medley
1 tablespoon garlic butter, more if needed
Salt and pepper to taste

Directions
1. Melt the butter in a cast-iron skillet over medium heat. To gauge the campfire's cooking temperature, simply do the hand test (page 9).
2. Cook for 15 minutes or until the vegetables are cooked through and juices have evaporated.
3. Season with salt and pepper to taste before serving.

Nutrition (per serving)
Calories 100, fat 1.5 g, carbs 5 g,
Protein 16 g, sodium 570 mg

Glazed Carrot

Glazed carrots are tender carrots mixed with a buttery glaze of butter, brown sugar, and white pepper.

Serves 6 | Prep. time 15 minutes | Cooking time 30 minutes

Ingredients
1 pound baby carrots, peeled
2 tablespoons butter
2 tablespoons packed brown sugar
Salt and pepper to taste
Chopped parsley, for garnish

Directions
1. Place the carrots in the cast-iron skillet. Cover with water and bring to boil over medium heat. To gauge the campfire's cooking temperature, simply do the hand test (page 9).
2. Cook for 10-12 minutes or until the carrots are tender. Remove from the skillet and drain the water. Transfer to a plate.
3. Melt the butter in the same cast-iron skillet. Stir in the brown sugar.
4. Add the carrots and cook for 5 minutes. Season with salt and pepper to taste.

5.   Sprinkle with chopped parsley and serve.

Nutrition (per serving)
Calories 124, fat 6 g, carbs 17 g, sugar 18 g,
Protein 1.1 g, sodium 193 mg

Corn Cakes

Corn cakes are a fluffy indulgent side dish loved by all ages. They're soft and fresh for chilly evenings. Enjoy with sour cream as an option.

Serves 4 | Prep. time 15 minutes | Cooking time 35 minutes

Ingredients
6 ounces cream cheese, softened
¼ cup butter, melted, more for greasing
6 large eggs
1 cup milk
1½ cups all-purpose flour
½ cup cornmeal
1 teaspoon baking powder
1 teaspoon salt
1 (15-ounce) can whole kernel corn, drained
¼ cup minced green onions
¼ cup vegetable oil, more if needed

Directions
1. Melt the butter in a cast-iron skillet over medium heat. To gauge the campfire's cooking temperature, simply do the hand test (page 9).

2. Let cool for a few minutes before pouring into a mixing bowl.
3. Add the cream cheese and mix well. Add the eggs and mix well.
4. Stir in the milk. Mix in the flour, cornmeal, baking powder, and salt.
5. Add the corn, salsa, and onions.
6. Warm the oil in the cast-iron skillet.
7. Working in batches not to over crowded the skillet, pour in ¼ cupfuls of the batter and cook until golden brown on both sides, about 5-7 minutes. Add and warm more oil if needed.

Nutrition (per serving)
Calories 334, fat 16 g, carbs 34 g, sugar 5 g,
Protein 11 g, sodium 715 mg

Stuffed Tomatoes

Serves 4 | Prep. time 10 minutes | Cooking time 30-32 minutes

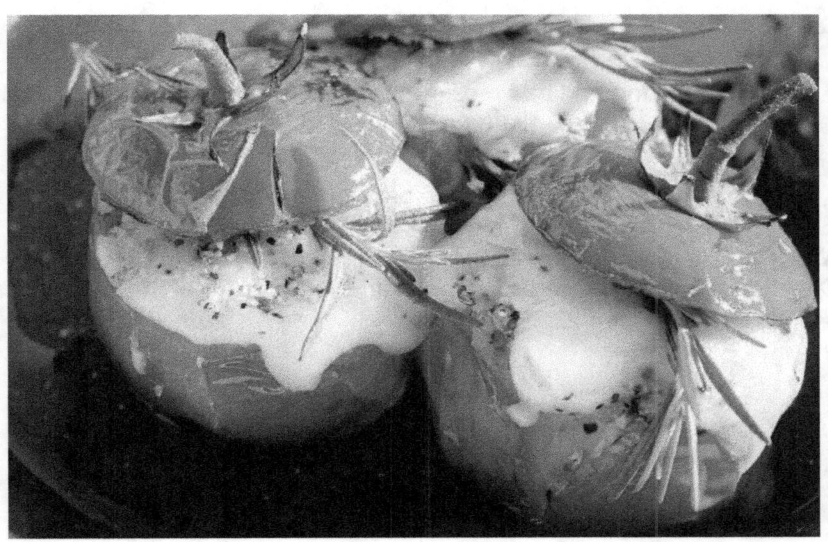

Ingredients
2 tablespoons cream cheese
1 tablespoon milk
½ cup shredded mozzarella cheese
4 cooked bacon slices, crumbled
½ cup leftover cooked rice
4 medium-sized tomatoes
Salt and pepper

Directions
1. Arrange the bacon slices in a cast-iron skillet, leaving some space between them.
2. Cook over medium heat for 10–12 minutes until crisp. To gauge the campfire's cooking temperature, simply do the hand test (page 9).
3. Let cool and drain over paper towels, then crumble.
4. Cut off the top of each tomato and hollow out the tomatoes to create space for stuffing.

5.   Add the cream cheese, rice, milk, and bacon to a mixing bowl. Combine well.
6.   Stuff the rice mixture into the tomatoes and place in the skillet.
7.   Add ½ cup of water to the bottom of the skillet around the tomatoes, top each tomato with their tops. Place on the grill over the campfire or over medium heat and let cook for 112-15 minutes, adding water if needed, or until tomatoes are cooked.
8.   Remove top and add mozzarella cheese. Continue cooking until the cheese melt, about 3-5 minutes. Season to taste with salt and pepper.
9.   To serve place top of tomato back on and serve warm.

Nutrition (per serving)
Calories 132, fat 10 g, carbs 4.5 g, sugar 0 g,
Protein 7 g, sodium 384 mg

Parmesan Brussels Sprouts

Serves 2 | Prep. time 10 minutes | Cooking time 15 minutes

Ingredients
2 cloves garlic, chopped
3 tablespoons butter, melted (divided)
12 Brussels sprouts, trimmed and halved
2 tablespoons shredded Parmesan cheese
Salt and ground black pepper to taste

Directions
1. Add 1 tablespoon of the butter to a cast-iron skillet and melt it over medium-high heat. To gauge the campfire's cooking temperature, simply do the hand test (page 9).
2. Add the garlic and stir-cook for about 30–40 seconds until softened and fragrant.
3. Melt another 1 tablespoon of the butter and add the Brussels sprouts, the cut-side down; stir and cover the skillet.
4. Allow to cook for 4–5 minutes. Flip the sprouts and add the final 1 tablespoon of butter.
5. Cover again and cook for 2–3 more minutes until browned.

6. Remove the skillet from the health add the Parmesan cheese on top and keep in the skillet for 2-3 minutes.
7. Season to taste with salt and pepper.

Nutrition (per serving)
Calories 203, fat 19 g, carbs 6.5 g, sugar 0g,
Protein 4 g, sodium 291 mg

Garlic Potatoes

Serves 6 | Prep. time 10 minutes | Cooking time 25 minutes

Ingredients
1 large onion, thinly sliced
1 red bell pepper, diced
3 tablespoons vegetable oil
6 medium red-skinned potatoes, cubed
2 teaspoons minced garlic
1 teaspoon ground paprika
½–1 teaspoon salt
Ground black pepper to taste

Directions
1. Add the oil to a cast-iron skillet and heat it over medium heat. To gauge the campfire's cooking temperature, simply do the hand test (page 9).
2. Add the sliced onion and stir-cook until softened and translucent.
3. Add the garlic and bell pepper; stir-cook for 1 minute.
4. Add the diced potatoes, salt, pepper and paprika; stir and cover the skillet.
5. Allow to cook for 10–15 minutes until the potatoes turn soft and tender.

6.   Uncover the skillet and increase heat to medium-high; cook for 8–10 more minutes until the potatoes are evenly brown, stirring occasionally.
7.   Season to taste and serve warm.

Nutrition (per serving)
Calories 161, fat 7 g, carbs 22 g, sugar 0 g,
Protein 3 g, sodium 400 mg

Cranberry Asparagus Nuts

Serves 4 | Prep. time 10 minutes | Cooking time 10 minutes

Ingredients
⅓ cup pine nuts
⅓ cup dried cranberries
1 bunch asparagus, trimmed ends
3 tablespoons olive oil
1 pinch salt

Directions
1. Add the oil to a cast-iron skillet and heat it over medium-high heat. To gauge the campfire's cooking temperature, simply do the hand test (page 9).
2. Add the cranberries, nuts and salt and stir-cook for 2-3 minutes until the nuts become golden. Transfer to a plate and set aside.
3. Add the asparagus spears; stir-cook for 6–8 minutes until the spears are bright green and fork tender.
4. Transfer to a serving plate, spoon the nuts and cranberries on top, and serve warm.

Nutrition (per serving)
Calories 206, fat 16 g, carbs 14 g, sugar 0 g
Protein 5 g, sodium 3 mg

Corn Casserole

Corn casserole is an easy and creamy casserole recipe. One of the best savory lunches for camping, it only has four ingredients: corn, heavy cream, butter, and salt and pepper for seasoning.

Serves 4 | Prep. time 10 minutes | Cooking time 25 minutes

Ingredients
4 ears corn
¼ cup salted butter
1½ cups heavy cream
Salt and pepper to taste

Directions
1. Remove the corn kernels into a bowl.
2. Heat the butter in a cast-iron skillet over medium-high heat. To gauge the campfire's cooking temperature, simply do the hand test (page 9).
3. Add the corn and toss well.
4. Add the heavy cream and season with salt and pepper.
5. Cook for 20 minutes, stirring a few time.

Nutrition (per serving)
Calories 150, fat 7 g, carbs 20 g, sugar 3.6 g,
Protein 3 g, sodium 314 mg

Spicy Green Beans

Spicy green beans are simple and nutritious as a side dish. They're made with garlic, soy sauce, red pepper flakes, and the sweetness of sugar.

Serves 4 | Prep. time 15 minutes | Cooking time 10 minutes

Ingredients
1 tablespoon vegetable oil, more if needed
2 cloves garlic, thinly sliced
1 pound green beans, trimmed
1 tablespoon sugar
2 tablespoons soy sauce
Red chili pepper flakes to taste

Directions
1. Heat the oil in a cast-iron skillet over medium-high heat. To gauge the campfire's cooking temperature, simply do the hand test (page 9).
2. Add the garlic and cook until light brown.
3. Add the green beans and cook for 5-8 minutes, until tender.
4. Mix in the sugar, and soy sauce and red chili pepper flakes.
5. Serve warm.

Nutrition (per serving)
Calories 72, fat 3 g, carbs 10 g, sugar 3 g,
Protein 1 g, sodium 140 mg

DESSERTS

S'mores in a Skillet

S'mores is a campfire favorite dessert. This skillet recipe will amaze everyone as your Graham crackers become a scoop for the gooey marshmallow and chocolate skillet.

Serves 4-6 | Prep. time 10 minutes | Cooking time 7 minutes

Ingredients
1 package graham crackers
2 cups mini marshmallows
2 cups semi-sweet chocolate chips

Directions
1. Light the barbecue grill or make a campfire. Melt the butter in a cast-iron skillet over medium heat. To gauge the campfire's cooking temperature, simply do the hand test (page 9).
2. Add the chocolate chips to the bottom of the skillet. Top with the marshmallows.

3. Place on the grill over the fire until the toppings melt and become gooey.
4. Scoop the s'mores melt with graham crackers and enjoy!

Nutrition (per serving)
Calories 345, fat 12 g, carbs 55 g, sugar 48 g
Protein 4 g, sodium 190 mg

Campfire Brownies

Simple, easy-to-make campfire brownies are here to make your dessert time special. A delightful and chocolaty treat to enjoy with your family on a fiery evening.

Serves 4 | Prep. time 10 minutes | Cooking time 10 minutes

Ingredients
1 box brownie mix
Mini marshmallows
⅓ cup chopped pecans, optional

Directions
1. Prepare the brownie mix according to the box directions. Add pecans to the batter, if desired.
4. Add the mix to a cast-iron skillet and cook over the campfire over medium heat for about 10-15 minutes until cooked through but still gooey. Melt the butter in a cast-iron skillet over medium heat. To gauge the campfire's cooking temperature, simply do the hand test (page 9).
2. Add the marshmallows on top. Cover carefully with a foil and cook for another 4-5 minutes until they melt.

Nutrition (per serving)
Calories 129, fat 4.6 g, carbs 21 g, sugar 12 g,
Protein 1.6 g, sodium 50 mg

Peanut Butter Bars

Peanut butter bars are chewy, crunchy, and heavenly tasting with minimal effort. They're ready in less than 30 minutes.

Serves 2 | Prep. time 10 minutes | Cooking time 15 minutes

Ingredients
1 tablespoon butter
2 cups icing sugar
1 cup peanut butter
1½ cups graham cracker crumbs
2 ounces semi-sweet chocolate

Directions
5. Melt the butter in a cast-iron skillet over medium-high heat. Melt the butter in a cast-iron skillet over medium heat. To gauge the campfire's cooking temperature, simply do the hand test (page 9).
1. Mix in the icing sugar, peanut butter, and graham cracker crumbs and spread the mixture over the skillet.

2.   Melt the chocolate over the campfire and spread it over the mixture in the skillet.
3.   Cooked for around 10-12 minutes.
4.   Remove from the skillet and let cool before slicing.

Nutrition (per serving)
Calories 150, fat 6 g, carbs 18 g, sugar 13 g,
Protein 6 g, sodium 80 mg

Apple French Toast

Apple French toast is a great dessert recipe and sweetly satisfying. It's easy to make in just 10 minutes with only four ingredients.

Serves 4 | Prep. time 10 minutes | Cooking time 25 minutes

Ingredients
4 tablespoons butter, divided
2 apples, cored, peeled, and sliced
2 eggs
4 thick sliced brioche bread
Cinnamon sugar for serving

Directions
1. Melt half of the butter in a cast-iron skillet over medium heat. To gauge the campfire's cooking temperature, simply do the hand test (page 9).
2. Add the apples to the skillet and stir fry until tender, about 5-8 minutes. Transfer to a plate and cover with foil to keep warm. Wipe skillet clean with paper towels.
3. Melt remaining butter.

4. Beat the eggs in a bowl. Dip the bread slices in the egg mixture, shake to remove excess egg mixture. Transfer to skillet and cook until golden brown on both sides, about 2-3 minutes per sides.
5. To serve, sprinkle the French toast with cinnamon sugar and top with some of the warm apples.

Nutrition (per serving)
Calories 310, fat 10 g, carbs 39 g, sugar 6 g,
Protein 16 g, sodium 32 mg

Maple Vanilla Custard

Serves 6 | Prep. time 10 minutes | Cooking time 10 minutes

Ingredients
4 large eggs
4 cups milk
1 teaspoon pure vanilla extract
½ cup maple syrup
½ teaspoon salt

Directions
1. Whisk eggs in bowl, mix in vanilla, maple syrup, and salt.
2. Pour milk into cast-iron pan. Bring to simmer over medium heat. To gauge the campfire's cooking temperature, simply do the hand test (page 9).
3. Remove milk from heat.
4. Add a tablespoon at a time of hot milk into egg mixture, mixing continuously in order not to cook egg.

5.   Once egg mixture has been tempered with milk, whisk egg mix-
     ture into pot of milk.
6.   Return pan to the heat and simmer for 5 minutes.
7.   Transfer to a bowl and let cool to serve.

Nutrition (per serving)
Calories 250, fat 6 g, carbs 38 g, sugar 2 g
Protein 11 g, sodium 147 mg

Chocolate Dump Cake

Serves 8 | Prep. time 10 minutes | Cooking time 35 minutes

Ingredients
1 (16-ounce) package chocolate cake mix
1 (3.9-ounce) package chocolate pudding mix
1 ½ cup milk
1 cup dark or semisweet chocolate chips
Butter for greasing or cooking spray

Directions
1. Lightly coat a large cast-iron skillet with a little butter or cooking spray.
2. In a bowl, combine milk, cake mix, pudding mix, and chocolate chips until you have a smooth thick batter.
3. Pour batter into the cast-iron skillet, cover with lid or foil.
4. Place over medium heat and cook covered for 30-40 minutes, until the cakes is cooked through. To gauge the campfire's cooking temperature, simply do the hand test (page 9).

Nutrition (per serving)
Calories 521, fat 15 g, carbs 58 g, sugar 3 g
Protein 3 g, sodium 240 mg

Walnut Chocolate Burritos

Walnut chocolate burritos are a simple and easy-to-make dessert that's ready in just 5 minutes. The chocolaty and gooey texture inside will suit your fancy.

Serves 4-8 | Prep. time 10 minutes | Cooking time 5 minutes

Ingredients
2 tablespoons butter
4 tortillas
1½ cups chocolate chips
1 cup chopped walnuts
1 cup marshmallows

Directions
1. Spread the butter over the tortillas.
2. Add the chocolate chips, walnuts, and marshmallows.
3. Wrap the tortillas around the filling ingredients.
6. Heat some butter in a cast-iron skillet over medium-high heat. Melt the butter in a cast-iron skillet over medium heat. To gauge the campfire's cooking temperature, simply do the hand test (page 9).
4. Cook the burritos for 2–3 minutes on each side.

Nutrition (per serving)
Calories 477, fat 30 g, carbs 58 g, sugar 31 g,
Protein 4.7 g, sodium 153 mg

RECIPE INDEX

APPENDIX

Cooking Conversion Charts

1. Measuring Equivalent Chart

Type	Imperial	Imperial	Metric
Weight	1 dry ounce		28g
	1 pound	16 dry ounces	0.45 kg
Volume	1 teaspoon		5 ml
	1 dessert spoon	2 teaspoons	10 ml
	1 tablespoon	3 teaspoons	15 ml
	1 Australian table-spoon	4 teaspoons	20 ml
	1 fluid ounce	2 tablespoons	30 ml
	1 cup	16 table-spoons	240 ml
	1 cup	8 fluid ounces	240 ml
	1 pint	2 cups	470 ml
	1 quart	2 pints	0.95 l
	1 gallon	4 quarts	3.8 l
Length	1 inch		2.54 cm

Numbers are rounded to the closest equivalent

2. Oven Temperature Equivalent Chart

Fahrenheit (°F)	Celsius (°C)	Gas Mark
220	100	
225	110	1/4
250	120	½
275	140	1
300	150	2
325	160	3
350	180	4
375	190	5
400	200	6
425	220	7
450	230	8
475	250	9
500	260	

*   Celsius (°C) = T (°F)-32] * 5/9
**   Fahrenheit (°F) = T (°C) * 9/5 + 32
*** Numbers are rounded to the closest equivalent

Internal Temperature Cooking Charts

Beef, Lamb, Roasts, Pork, Veal, Ham

Rare	120 – 130°F (49 – 54°C)
Medium Rare	130 – 135°F (54 – 57°C)
Medium	135 – 145°F (57 – 63°C)
Medium Well	145 – 155°F (64 – 68°C)
Well Done	155°F and greater (68°C)

Pork, ribs

Fully Cooked	190 – 205°F (88 – 96°C)

Poultry

Fully Cooked	At least 165°F (74°C)

Fish

Fully Cooked	At least 130°F (54°C)

F=Fahrenheit; C=Celcius